THE LITTLE GUIDE TO

PRINCE

First published in 2019

This edition published in 2023 by OH!
An Imprint of Welbeck Non-Fiction Limited,
part of Welbeck Publishing Group.
Offices in: London – 20 Mortimer Street, London W1T 3JW
and Sydney – Level 17, 207 Kent St, Sydney NSW 2000 Austraia
www.welbeckpublishing.com

Compilation text © Welbeck Non-Fiction Limited 2023
Design © Welbeck Non-Fiction Limited 2023

Disclaimer:

ISBN 978-1-80069-509-2

Compiled and written by: Malcolm Croft
Editorial: Ross Hamilton
Project manager: Russell Porter
Production: Jess Brisley

A CIP catalogue record for this book is available from the British Library

Printed in China

10 9 8 7 6 5 4 3 2 1

THE LITTLE GUIDE TO
PRINCE

WISDOM AND WONDER FROM
THE LOVESEXY SUPERSTAR

CONTENTS

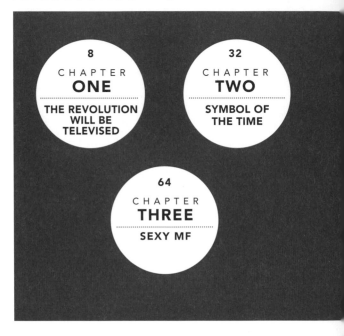

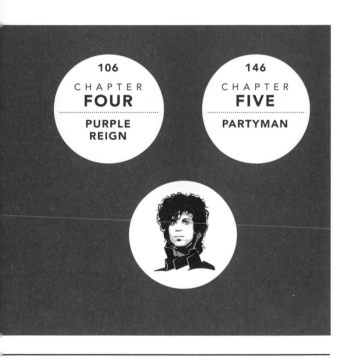

106

CHAPTER
FOUR

PURPLE
REIGN

146

CHAPTER
FIVE

PARTYMAN

INTRODUCTION

Little did the world know on June 7, 1958, that the future king – well, Prince, to use his birth name – of rock and roll would be five feet two inches tall, sing in a register usually only enjoyed by puppies, and have a penchant for all things purple. Prince made sticking out like a sore thumb look sexy and cool without ever seeming like he was trying that hard.

In his tenure at the top of the pops, from his first self-produced record *For You* (1978) to his global monster album and film *Purple Rain* (1984) and beyond, Prince may have performed under a plethora of names, but the world's first proper pop mononym was beloved for being just one thing: the bridge that united pop, funk, soul, dance, jazz and rock in a way the world had never heard before. Or since.

Prince's early days growing up in a "black and white world" in Minnesota may have been as dysfunctional as those of many other 80s rock icons, but that's where any colourless clichés stop dead. As soon as Prince Rogers Nelson broke ground on his first record in 1978, the gloves came off and on squeezed the high heels and crushed velvet catsuits. You could not hold the man, or his music, back.

Dearly beloved, we gather together for this book to enjoy that thing called Prince's life. With His Highness gone, all that is left of the man today is his timeless music. As he was never one for interviews, this collection of quotes and quips stands as a last will and testament of a musician who will long be revered as a one-of-a-kind, irreplaceable talent. The genuine article; the real deal: there will never be another quite like him. If music can be embodied by just one man, Prince be thy name. Enjoy!

CHAPTER

ONE

THE REVOLUTION WILL BE TELEVISED

From his first hit, 1978's "Soft and Wet", through to his final one, 2015's "Free Urself" – and the (almost) 100 singles in between – the Artist Forever Known As Prince was consistently unparalleled in his majesty. No one dared compare to him.

Here, in his own unforgettable words, let's find out why he was the best…

Everybody always stops talking or doing anything when I walk in! They say it's the artist who changes, but, I don't know, I really think it's everybody else.

Prince, on fame changing him, interview with Smokey D. Fontaine, *Medium* magazine, September 2, 2015.

The most important thing is to be true to yourself, but I also like danger. That's what's missing from pop music today. There's no excitement or mystery.

Prince, about the stale state of pop music, interview with Richard Harrington, *Washington Post*, July 29, 1984.

The key to longevity is to learn every aspect of music that you can.

Prince, about learning his craft, said live on
The View TV Show, 2010.

All people care about
nowadays is getting paid,
so they try to do just what
the audience wants them to
do. I'd rather give people
what they need rather than
just what they want.

Prince, on giving his audience what they want,
interview with Robert Hilburn, *Los Angeles Times*,
November 21, 1982.

Like books and black lives, albums still matter.

99

Prince, on the importance of albums, said live on TV at the 57th Grammy Awards, February 8, 2015.

66

I was brought up in a black and white world. I dig black and white; night and day, rich and poor, man and woman. I listen to all kinds of music and I want to be judged on the quality of my work, not on what I say, nor on what people claim I am, nor on the colour of my skin.

99

Prince, on being judged, article in *Guitar World* magazine, October 1988.

In a legacy beaming with way too many awards and acclaim to mention, Prince also had the sales figures to prove his power and influence over the next generation.

Across his 40-year career, and 42 studio albums, Prince sold more than 100 million records.

"

Each song writes itself. It's already perfect.

Prince, on the songs writing themselves, interview with
Robert L. Doerschuk, *Musician* magazine, April 1997.

A lot of times I didn't know I was pushing the envelope until later. In today's climate you've got everybody thinking that that's a holy grail to do something explicit. And what happens is it's not explicit anymore because everybody's doing it.

Prince, on pushing the envelope, interview with Matt Lauer *Today Show*, March 19, 2004.

I can't help but be sexy. I mean, that's just what it is. You know, sex isn't so much what you say. It's how you say it and the way you sing, you know? It just comes out that way.

Prince, on being sexy, interview with Matt Lauer *Today Show*, March 19, 2004.

I would ask people who want to call this record a comeback where they think I'm coming back from.

Prince, on his "comeback" with his *Musicology* album, interview with *CBS News*, May 3, 2004.

When you show you can be successful as an independent artist, the umbilical cord is broken. Record contracts are a parent–child relationship. An advance is an allowance.

Prince, on record contracts, interview with *Associated Press*, May 2004.

Sometimes I hear a melody in my head, and it seems like the first colour in a painting. And then you can build the rest of the song with other added sounds. You just have to try to be with that first colour, like a baby yearns to come to its parents. That's why creating music is really like giving birth.

Prince, on his songwriting craft, interview with *Guitar World* magazine, October 1998.

Music is like the universe: the sounds are like the planets, the air and the light fitting together.

Prince, on music, interview with *Guitar World* magazine, October 1998.

My bassist, Sonny T., can play a girl's measurements on his instrument and make you see them. I love the idea of visual sounds.

Prince, on seeing sounds, interview with *Guitar World* magazine, October 1998.

When I wrestled with demons, I had moods when I couldn't figure something out and so I ran to vice to sort myself out, like women or too much drink, or working in order to avoid dealing with the problem.

Prince, on his demons and vices, interview with *Guitar World* magazine, October 1998.

Attention to detail makes the difference between a good song and a great song. And I meticulously try to put the right sound in the right place, even sounds that you would only notice if I left them out.

Prince, on what makes a good song great, interview with *Guitar World* magazine, October 1998.

Prince Rogers Nelson is on my birth certificate. My father wanted me to be a star, so he named me Prince.

Prince, on nominative determinism, interview with *Ebony* magazine, January 1997.

Writers often use the word 'prolific' with me, but I don't think that's right. When you're committed to something like we are, when you spend the amount of time on something that we do, then you're bound to create a lot. This is what we do. This is our job.

Prince, on his prolificness, interview with Smokey D. Fontaine, *Medium* magazine, September 2, 2015.

Everyone has their own experience. That's why we are here, to go through our experience, to learn, to godown those paths and eventually you may have gone down so many paths and learned so much that you don't have to come back again.

Prince, on life, interview with Sylvia Paterson, *NME* magazine, October 1996.

"

When I was younger, I had a massive ego. *Massive.* But that's not such a bad thing. Because at least you're aspiring to be something, you consider yourself great because you want to be great.

"

Prince, on his massive ego, interview with Sylvia Paterson, *NME* magazine, October 1996.

When I became a symbol, all the writers were cracking funnies, but I was the one laughing. I knew I'd be here today, feeling as if each new album is my first.

Prince, on changing his name, interview with Lorraine Ali, *Newsweek*, April 12, 2004.

CHAPTER

TWO

SYMBOL OF THE TIME

Prince may have burst onto the music scene at the same time as another culture-baiting mononym – we're looking at you, Madonna! – but he was completely on his own in regards to his output, both prolific and innovative at the same time.

A true original, Prince's musical funkiness was not only the soundtrack of the 1980s – it defined the time too. He was, literally, the sign of his times.

I didn't let fame rule me.

Prince, on fame, interview with Mick Brown,
the *Telegraph*, April 2004.

You only get famous once.
The audience you have is the
audience you always have.

Prince, on fame, interview with Mick Brown,
the *Telegraph*, April 2004.

Really, I'm normal. A little highly strung, maybe. But normal. But so much has been written about me and people never know what's right and what's wrong. I'd rather let them stay confused.

Prince, on being normal, interview with Mick Brown, the *Telegraph*, April 2004.

Music is everything to me. I love making music. I am making music. Music is spirit, it's therapy. It makes me feel a certain way, and if played with conviction and soul, the same thing occurs in other people.

Prince, on music's importance, interview with Mick Brown, the *Telegraph*, April 2004.

Prince is dead. [Warner Bros. Records] killed him. I don't own Prince's music. If you don't own your masters, your master owns you.

Prince, on the music industry, interview with *Rolling Stone*, October 1996.

Musicians inherited this system, so that's how most musicians work, how we get the music to the people. But it used to be the tradition to have slaves on the plantation. Don't mean it's right!

Prince, on not owning his master recordings, interview with *Rolling Stone*, October 1996.

66

I'm no different to anyone. Yes, I have fame and wealth and talent, but I certainly don't consider myself any better than anyone who has no fame, wealth or talent. People fascinate me. Life fascinates me! And I'm no more fascinated by my own life than by anyone else's.

99

Prince, on his talent, interview with Sylvia Paterson, *NME* magazine, October 1996.

I ran away from home when I was 12. I've changed address in Minneapolis 32 times, and there was a great deal of loneliness. But when I think about it, I know I'm here for a purpose, and I don't worry about it so much.

Prince, on his upbringing, interview with Bill Adler, *Rolling Stone*, February 19, 1981.

I don't need no producer, I don't need no record company, no A&R man or anyone telling me what to do. I produce my own records in my own studio. Why do I need someone telling me what to do, and owning what I do?

Prince, on being independent, interview with Mick Brown, the *Telegraph*, April 2004.

I don't let computers use me. It's more interesting to me to pick up a guitar and create a sound out of thin air. That's analogue. We're analogue creatures; we breathe air, we hear soundwaves, we react to spirit and colour. A computer's binary.

Prince, on remaining analogue in a digital world, interview with Mick Brown, the *Telegraph*, April 2004.

Prince's side hustle was writing hits for other artists. Here's ten of his very best…

1. The Bangles –
"Manic Monday" (1986)

2. Sinead O'Connor –
"Nothing Compares 2 U" (1990)

3. Stevie Nicks –
"Stand Back" (1983)

4. Alicia Keys –
"How Come You Don't Call Me" (2001)

5. Madonna –
"Love Song" (1989)

6. Chaka Khan –
"I Feel For You" (1984)

7. Sheena Easton –
"Sugar Walls" (1984)

8. Cyndi Lauper –
"When You Were Mine" (1983)

9. Martika –
"Love... Thy Will Be Done" (1991)

10. Kate Bush –
"Why Should I Love You?" (1993)

I do feel like a punk, because no one believes in God anymore.

Prince, on religion, interview with Sylvia Paterson, *NME* magazine, October 1996.

If you put a loaf of bread on the table, it turns into medicine and to me that is incredible. The bread will eventually take care of itself. That's nature, that's the Truth.

Prince, on the Truth, interview with Sylvia Paterson, *NME* magazine, October 1996.

I know those paths of excess, drugs, sex and alcohol – all those experiences can be funky, they can be very funky, but they're just paths, a diversion, not the answer…

Prince, on excess, interview with Sylvia Paterson, *NME* magazine, October 1996.

I find freedom sexy. I find freedom so sexy I can't even explain it to you. You wake up every day and feel like you can do anything.

Prince, on freedom, interview with Sylvia Paterson, *NME* magazine, October 1996.

I was constantly running from family to family. It was nice on one hand, because I always had a new family, but I didn't like being shuffled around. I was a bitter kid for a while, but I adjusted.

Prince, on his upbringing, interview with Debby Miller, *Rolling Stone*, April 28, 1983.

Everything about my music
is autobiographical.

Prince, on his music, interview with Tony Mitchell,
Sounds magazine, June 6, 1981.

Dirty Mind really felt like me for once. When I brought it to the record company it shocked a lot of people. But they didn't ask me to go back and change anything, and I'm really grateful. I wasn't being deliberately provocative… I was being deliberately me.

Prince, on the *Dirty Mind* album, interview with Tony Mitchell, *Sounds* magazine, June 6, 1981.

I hear things in my sleep;
I walk around and go to the
bathroom and try to brush
my teeth and all of a sudden
the toothbrush starts
vibrating! That's a groove!

Prince, on inspiration, radio interview with The Electrifying
Mojo, Detroit WHYT, June 7, 1986.

People think I'm a crazy fool for writing 'slave' on my face. But if I can't do what I want to do, what am I? When you stop a man from dreaming, he becomes a slave. That's where I was.

Prince, on SLAVE face writing, interview with Anthony DeCurtis, *Rolling Stone* magazine, October 17, 1996.

I'm not the Artist Formerly Known as Anything. Use my name.

Prince, on changing his name, article published on The Current.org, February 20, 2017.

I'm not saying I'm better than anybody else. But I'll be sitting there at the Grammys, and U2 will beat you. And you say to yourself, 'Wait a minute. I can play that kind of music. But they can't do 'Housequake'.

Prince, on being unique, interview with Neal Karlen, *Rolling Stone* magazine, October 18, 1990.

56

You know when you buy someone's record and there's always an element missing? The voice is wrong or the drums are lame or something? On mine there's nothing missing.

Prince, on perfection, interview with Chris Heath, *The Face* magazine, December 1991.

I make music because if I don't, I'd die. I record because it's in my blood. I hear sounds all the time. It's almost a curse: to know you can always make something new.

Prince, on making music, interview with Chris Heath, *The Face* magazine, December 1991.

I play a lot of styles. This is not arrogance; this is the truth. Sometimes I just stand in awe of what I do myself. I feel like a regular person, but I listen to *Emancipation* and wonder, 'Where did it come from?'

Prince, on the creation of his style, interview with Jon Pareles, *New York Times*, November 17, 1996.

Prince was known by many nicknames in his illustrious career. From the love symbol glyph to TAFKAP (The Artist Formerly Known As Prince), The Purple One, The Dude, Alexander Nevermind and Joey Coco to Jamie Starr, Christopher, Tora Tora, Skipper, High Priest of Pop, His Royal Badness and the Prince of Funk. His birth name was Prince Rogers Nelson.

I think when one discovers himself he discovers God. Or maybe it's the other way around.

Prince, on being unique, interview with Neal Karlen, *Rolling Stone* magazine, October 18, 1990.

Music was put on earth
to enlighten and empower
us and feel closer to our
centre.

"

Prince, on the power of music, interview with
Guitar World magazine, October 1998.

There's an incredible peace in my life now and I'm trying to share it with people.

Prince, on life in his fifties, interview with Peter Willis, *Daily Mirror*, July 5, 2010.

CHAPTER

THREE

SEXY MF

From his alluring stage costumes
to his iconic guitar playing, his desire
for the colour purple to his full-on
24/7 horniness, as heard in pretty
much every lyric he ever wrote,
Prince squished together the
boundaries of sex and music to make
a sound that positively screamed
with orgasmic delight.

Mind your step, it's about to get
soft and wet...

Larry King asked me once, 'Didn't you need a record company to make it?' But that has nothing to do with it. You don't need a record company to turn you into anything. I had autonomous control from the very beginning.

Prince, on record labels, interview with Alexis Petridis, *The Guardian*, November 12, 2015.

You know how easy it would have been to just put it in a different key? That would have shut everybody up who said the album wasn't half as powerful! I don't want to make an album like the earlier ones, you dig?

Prince, on "Raspberry Beret", interview with Neal Karlen, *Rolling Stone* magazine, October 18, 1985.

I don't want to be the CEO of anything. No titles. The minute you've accepted a title you're a slave to it. You're no longer free. The more people you allow to come between you and your music, the further it moves away from you. This isn't your business, it's your life.

Prince, on being nobody's slave, interview with Ben Edwards, *Mojo* magazine, August 1998.

The more I think about it, the more music is all just based on colours and sounds. Miles Davis wasn't thinking in terms of bridging. People wanted to play with him because they knew he wasn't going to bow to any rules. A strong spirit transcends rules.

Prince, on breaking the rules, interview with Barney Hoskyns, *Mojo* magazine, March 2000.

More than anything else,
I try not to repeat myself.
It's the hardest thing in the
world to do – there's only
so many notes one human
being can muster.

Prince, on repetition, interview with Neal Karlen,
Rolling Stone magazine, October 18, 1985.

When a person does get a hit, they try to do it again the same way. I don't think I've ever done that. I think that's the problem with the music industry today.

Prince, on recreating a hit, interview with Neal Karlen, *Rolling Stone* magazine, October 18, 1985.

People describe me as a loving tyrant. I'm probably the hardest bandleader to work for, but I do it for love.

Prince, on being a bandleader, interview with Dorian Lynsky, *The Guardian*, June 23, 2011.

Purple Rain was 100 shows, and around the 75th, I went crazy.

Prince, on *Purple Rain*, interview with Dorian Lynsky, *The Guardian*, June 23, 2011.

Prince died on April 21, 2016, at the age of just 57. The cause of his death was announced as an accidental overdose of the drug fentanyl (none of the pills found were prescribed to him).

With no heir, and no will, more than 700 people claimed to be half-siblings or descendants of the artist in order to seize control of his multi-million-dollar estate.

The challenge is to outdo what I've done in the past. I play each show as if it's the last one.

Prince, on playing live, interview with Dorian Lynsky, *The Guardian*, June 23, 2011.

I love growing older. The older
I get the closer I am to where I'm
going, which is a better place.
We all have a purpose within us.
We are put here for a reason.
My talent is God-given, but the
music is made by me. I make the
choices that make the music.

Prince, on growing older, interview with David Sinclair,
The Times, December 22, 1996.

66

If I need psychological evaluation, I'll do it myself.

99

Prince, on pyschotherapy, interview with Dorian Lynsky, *The Guardian*, June 23, 2011.

The sooner this thing called fame goes away, the better. We got people who don't need to be famous. 🙰

Prince, on fame, interview with Dorian Lynsky, *The Guardian*, June 23, 2011.

I had some old clothes on because I was going to help a friend move house and some girls came by and one went: 'Oh-my-god, Prince!' And the other girl pulled a face and said, 'That ain't Prince.' I didn't come out of the house raggedy after that.

Prince, on fame, interview with Dorian Lynsky, *The Guardian*, June 23, 2011.

Michael Jackson and I both came along at a time when there was nothing. MTV didn't have anyone who was visual. Bowie, maybe. A lot of people made great records but dressed like they were going to the supermarket.

Prince, on dressing for success, interview with Dorian Lynsky, *The Guardian*, June 23, 2011.

How many people have substance and how many are just putting on crazy clothes?

Prince, on style over substance, interview with Dorian Lynsky, *The Guardian*, June 23, 2011.

"

Well, I don't think it. I know it.

"

Prince, when asked "Do you think you're good?",
interview with Dorian Lynsky, *The Guardian*, June 23, 2011.

Anyone who was around back then knew what was happening. When they were sleeping, I was jamming. I was working. When they woke up, I had another groove. I'm as insane that way now as I was back then.

Prince, on his prolificness, interview with Neal Karlen, *Rolling Stone* magazine, October 18, 1990.

Half the things people were writing about me were true.

Prince, on the press, interview with Neal Karlen, *Rolling Stone* magazine, October 18, 1990.

Cool means being able to hang with yourself. All you have to ask yourself is 'Is there anybody I'm afraid of? Is there anybody who if I walked into a room and saw, I'd get nervous?' If not, then you're cool.

Prince, on what it means to be cool, interview with Neal Karlen, *Rolling Stone* magazine, October 18, 1990.

It is believed there are more than 8,000 songs written and recorded by Prince that have never been officially released from his Paisley Park vault.

That is enough material to release a new album every year…for 100 years!

66

You can always renegotiate a record contract. You just go in and say, 'You know, I think my next project will be a Country & Western album.'

99

Prince, on record contracts, interview with Neal Karlen, *Rolling Stone* magazine, October 18, 1990.

I am what I am. I feel if I can please myself musically, then I can please others, too.

Prince, on what pleases him, interview with Neal Karlen, *Rolling Stone* magazine, October 18, 1990.

Some might not get it.
But people also said *Purple Rain* was unreleasable.
And now I drive to work each morning to my own big studio.

Prince, on *Purple Rain*, interview with Neal Karlen, *Rolling Stone* magazine, October 18, 1990.

I'm not trying to be this great visionary wizard. Perfection is in everyone. It's not just something that I have the keys to. Nobody's perfect, but they can be. We may never reach that, but it's better to strive than not.

Prince, on perfection, interview with Neal Karlen, *Rolling Stone* magazine, September 12, 1985.

66

You've got to understand that there's only so much you can do on an electric guitar. There are only so many sounds a guitar can make. Lord knows I've tried to make a guitar sound like something new to myself.

99

Prince, on electric guitars, interview with Neal Karlen, *Rolling Stone* magazine, September 12, 1985.

Prince's bestselling album was, of course, 1984's *Purple Rain* soundtrack. It sold a staggering 25 million copies and includes the decade-defining tracks 'Purple Rain' and 'When Doves Cry'.

On the day of the titular movie's release, June 25, 1984, Prince held the top spot at the U.S. box office, singles chart and album chart.

Today, people don't write songs; they're a lot of sounds, a lot of repetition. That happened when producers took over, and that's why there's no more live acts. There's no box office anymore. The producers took over, and now nobody wants to see these bands.

Prince, on modern studio production, interview with Neal Karlen, *Rolling Stone* magazine, September 12, 1985.

Kids save a lot of money for a long time to buy tickets, and I like to give them what they want. When I was a kid, I didn't want to go hear James Brown play something I never heard before. I wanted to hear him play something I knew, |so I could dance.

Prince, on giving the audience what they want, interview with Neal Karlen, *Rolling Stone* magazine, October 18, 1990.

Mick Jagger said he hoped he wouldn't be singing 'Satisfaction' at thirty, and he's still singing it. Pete Townshend wrote, 'Hope I die before I get old.' Well, now he is old, and I do hope he's happy to be around. I don't want to say anything that can be held against me later!

Prince, on not singing anything he'll regret later, interview with Neal Karlen, *Rolling Stone* magazine, October 18, 1990.

66

When I pray to God, I say,
'It's your call – when it's
time to go, it's time to go.
But as long as you're going
to leave me here, then
I'm going to cause much
ruckus!'

99

Prince, on living life out loud, interview with Neal Karlen,
Rolling Stone magazine, October 18, 1990.

The first line in that song is 'Your butt is mine'. Now, I was saying to Michael, 'Who's gonna sing that to whom? 'Cause you sure ain't singin' that to me! And I sure ain't singin' that to you. Right there, we got a problem.'

Prince, on Michael Jackson, interview with Chris Rock, VH121, 1997.

The internet's like MTV. At one time MTV was hip and suddenly it became outdated. Anyway, all these computers and digital gadgets are no good. They just fill your head with numbers and that can't be good for you.

Prince, on the internet, interview with Matt Wilkinson, *NME*, July 5, 2010.

Record contracts are just like – I'm gonna say the word – slavery. I would tell any young artist… don't sign.

Prince, on record contracts, article posted by NPR.org, August 9, 2015.

The music I make a lot of the time is reflective of the life I am leading.

Prince, on his life as inspiration, interview with Spike Lee, *Interview* magazine, May 1997.

When you wake up, each day looks the same, so each day should be a new beginning. I don't have an expiration date.

Prince, on his life philosophy, interview with Anthony DeCurtis, *Rolling Stone* magazine, May 17, 2004.

Listen to *Emancipation* and you will hear what a free man sounds like.

Prince, on his emancipation from Warner Bros. record label, interview with Chris Rock, VH121, 1997.

You give a man a million dollars, he's a millionaire. But there is still higher to go, isn't there? You give someone like me all he's ever wanted, which is a recording studio, and that's it, right? There is nothing else for me to get, nothing else to buy.

Prince, on Paisley Park, interview with *New Zealand Herald*, November 14, 1996.

I hope to see the day that all men are free and can make things as free men, whether it's a building, a car or a neighbourhood. How would our neighbourhoods be? What would we do in a perfect world where we are completely free?

Prince, on the future, interview with *New Zealand Herald*, November 14, 1996.

I play a diverse range of styles, I always have, and it's really hard to do everything that you are feeling on one album of nine songs. I just do too much.

Prince, on his genre-bending range, interview with *New Zealand Herald*, November 14, 1996.

CHAPTER

FOUR

PURPLE REIGN

Prince was dipped head to toe in 24-carat purple for most of his forty-year career. No other artist before him, or since, was so famously devoted, and distracted, by a single colour. But it was just one of many distinct features that defined the artist. Prince was a rainbow of curiousity.

From his emancipation from Warner Bros. to his symbolic name-change, his legendary live performances to his now-iconic interviews, Prince never held back…and the colour purple was there by his side throughout, a protective prop to ensure his purple reign at the top could never be stopped…

The record business is like *The Matrix.* All the levels keep dissolving until you can't see what's behind anything. I'm not against the record industry. Their system is perfect. It benefits the people who it was designed to benefit: the owners.

Prince, on the music industry, interview with Beth Coleman, *Paper* magazine, June 1999.

I was never rich, so Ihave very little regard for money now. I only respect it inasmuch as it can feed somebody. I give a lot of it away. Money is best spent on someone who needs it. That's all I'm going to say. I don't like to make a big deal about it.

Prince, on his wealth, interview with Neal Karlen, *Rolling Stone* magazine, September 12, 1985.

Prince rose as high as the heavens musically, but his height was much more diminutive: five feet, two inches. (The same as Napoleon.)

The reason I didn't use other musicians on my records a lot of the time had to do with the hours that I worked. I swear to God it's not out of boldness when I say this, but there's not a person around who can stay awake as long as I can. Music is what keeps me awake.

Prince, on working late, interview with Neal Karlen, *Rolling Stone* magazine, September 12, 1985.

I don't look for whether something's cool or not. If I do something that I think belongs to someone else or sounds like someone else, I do something else.

Prince, on being original, interview with Neal Karlen, *Rolling Stone* magazine, September 12, 1985.

One of the several hundred unreleased records in the Paisley Park vaults is *Camille*. This album was originally recorded in 1986 under the pseudonym Camille, a female alter ego portrayed by Prince.

The album's songs are sung in Prince's normal vocal register but then altered in production using pitch-shifting technology to an androgynous register.

Record companies are run by men who think they run America. They think they're the smartest but they're not. They don't know what's going on in my mind.

Prince, on record companies, his first interview with Andy Richardson, *NME*, March 11, 1995.

Once the internet is a reality the music business is finished. There won't be any need for record companies. If I can send you my music direct, what's the point of having a music business?

Prince, on the internet, his first interview with Andy Richardson, *NME*, March 11, 1995.

As the millennium approaches, we all must look inward and speak the truth. I had a boss, and I didn't like it. No more than you like it. I feel free now that there's no daddy around to spank me. It's time for us to stand up for what we believe in.

Prince, on speaking the truth, his first interview with Touré, *Icon* magazine, October 1998.

You don't know how much it hurts not owning your own material. When a record company goes ahead and does something with a song you wrote… it can make you angry for a week.

Prince, on not owning his own music, his first interview with Touré, *Icon* magazine, October 1998.

I follow what God tells me to do. He said, 'Change your name,' and I changed my name to a symbol ready for internet use before I knew anything about the internet.

Prince, on changing his name, interview with Larry King, CNN, July 1999.

I've always dressed the way I've wanted to and if it goes with the music, it's only because the music is part of me and so is the way I dress. I don't try to do anything to shock people or to make money – that would make me a hooker.

Prince, on his fashion sense, interview with Steve Sutherland, *Melody Maker*, June 6, 1981.

119

Prince wrote his first song on his father's piano when he was just seven years old.

It was called "Funk Machine", naturally.

People's perception of me changed after *Purple Rain*, and it pigeonholed me. I saw kids coming to concerts who screamed just because that's where the audience screamed in the movie. That's why I did 'Around the World in a Day', to totally change that. I wanted not to be pigeonholed.

Prince, on being pigeonholed, interview with *Entertainment Weekly*, May 28, 1999.

I know that people want to talk about the past. We're not at 'Purple Rain' anymore. We don't look like that, we don't dress like that, we're different people now. If you talk about that, the next thing you know, people start writing things like the Revolution is going to reunite!

Prince, on moving on from the past, interview with *Entertainment Weekly*, May 28, 1999.

Record companies expect their artists to lose their voice, their hair and their energy. I'm not doing any of that.

Prince, on defying expectations, interview with *Entertainment Weekly*, May 28, 1999.

Malcolm X thinks differently than Malcolm Little [his birth name]. When you're trying to change, you have to divorce yourself from the past.

Prince, on Malcolm X, interview with Vickie Gilmer, *Minneapolis Star Tribune*, September 3, 1999.

I skipped school a lot, but I graduated early; dismissal was my favourite time of day. I believe in teachers, but not for me. Anything creative I don't think can be taught, otherwise you get somebody else's style; it's not yours, it's theirs.

Prince, on his childhood, interview with Jon Bream, *Minneapolis Star*, January 5, 1979.

I'm a writer. Stephen King is a writer. Can I take a page out of his book and call it Prince's *Shining*? Can I take a scene out of a movie and call it my own? They say the law helps the writers. I don't need help; I don't need your money. Let us steward our own music.

Prince, on being a writer, interview with Jeff Jensen, *Entertainment Weekly*, April 23, 2004.

It took me four albums to get on the cover of *Rolling Stone*. Now it takes new artists only one. There should be rules for that kind of thing!

Prince, on the media, interview with Jeff Jensen, *Entertainment Weekly*, April 23, 2004.

Paisley Park is the place one should find in oneself, where one can go when one is alone.

Prince, on Paisley Park, interview with Neal Karlen, *Rolling Stone* magazine, September 12, 1985.

All these hip-hop artists today, the first thing they do is start their own label and lock their business down – I had a lot to do with that.

Prince, on modern hip-hop artists, interview with Anthony DeCurtis, *Rolling Stone* magazine, May 27, 2004.

I saw myself as an instrumentalist who started singing out of necessity. To me, my voice is just like one of the instruments I play. It's just one thing I do.

Prince, on his voice, interview with Jeff Schneider, *Insider* magazine, May 1978.

In 2016, the year of his death, Prince became the biggest-selling artist of the year, shifting more than one million records in one day!

I like the ones with nice personalities.

"

Prince, on women, interview with Cynthia Horner, *Right On!* magazine, December 1979.

By the time I was a sophomore, school had gotten to be a real drag. I was getting further and further into making music. The more I found myself entertaining at local gigs during the night, the more I hated the thought of going to school in the morning.

Prince, on his time at school, interview with Jeff Schneider, *Insider* magazine, May 1978.

I'm not entangled in a bunch of lawsuits and a web that I can't get out of. I can hold my head up... a happily married man who has his head in order. There isn't a bunch of scandal in my life.

Prince, on keeping clean of tabloid scandals, interview with Nekesa Mumbi Moody, CBS News, May 3, 2004.

I always knew I had a relationship with God. But I wasn't sure God had a relationship with me.

Prince, on religion, interview with Nekesa Mumbi Moody, CBS News, May 3, 2004.

No one can come and claim ownership of my work. I am the creator of it, and it lives within me.

Prince, on ownership of his music, interview with Jon Pareles, *New York Times*, July 12, 2004.

66

I was seventeen, a graduate and frustrated. I felt that I had to keep going after the music but didn't know how long I'd be able to do it and eat too. I did know that I wanted something more than just a nine to five.

99

Prince, on his time at school, interview with Jeff Schneider, *Insider* magazine, May 1978.

Embarrassed? I don't know that word. Have you seen my outfits?

Prince, on his fashion sense, interview with Jon Pareles, *New York Times*, July 12, 2004.

> **"**
> What it all boils down to means nothing except love. As long as I got that, I don't need money. If I went broke, it wouldn't faze me. Love and music. As long as I got that, everything's cool. Everything.
> **"**

Prince, on what's really important, interview with Jon Bream, *Minneapolis Star*, January 4, 1979.

Once you learn piano, everything else falls into place.

Prince, on learning piano, interview with Tony Mitchell, *Sounds* magazine, June 6, 1981.

I'm only a conductor of
whatever electricity comes
from the world, or wherever
we all come from. To me the
ultimate responsibility
is the hardest one –
the responsibility to be
true to myself.

Prince, on being true to himself, interview with Tony
Mitchell, *Sounds* magazine, June 6, 1981.

It's all just part of the
dream factory. If it happens,
it happens. It's best not
to even worry about that,
'cause if you strive for it
and don't get it, you'll be
disappointed and feel like
a failure.

Prince, on musical success, interview with Jon Bream,
Minneapolis Star, January 4, 1979.

66

If it wasn't against the law,
I wouldn't wear anything.

99

Prince, on his stage costumes, interview with
Chris Salewicz, *Melody Maker*, June 6, 1981.

I find it a lot easier to sing swear words than to say them and when I first had a girl, I found it really hard to tell my mother but, Lord knows, I didn't feel embarrassed while I was doing it to her.

Prince, on swearing, interview with Chris Salewicz, *Melody Maker*, June 6, 1981.

I don't want to just be doing what's expected of me. I just want to live… until it's time to die…

Prince, on living life to the fullest, interview with Chris Salewicz, *Melody Maker*, June 6, 1981.

CHAPTER

FIVE

PARTYMAN

Prince was beloved by millions of adoring fans for his everlasting ability to look like he was having all the fun all the time. His seriousness was only ever matched by his silliness.

The Joker to his own Batman, Prince was a symbol. More than just a man, he was an incorruptible icon that could strike fun into the hearts of those who followed him with just one thrust of his purple plectrum. He was the superhero the world always needed when things got a little too serious.

He was the Partyman. And the party ain't over yet…

People call me a prodigy. I don't even know what the word really means. I'm just a person.

Prince, on being called a prodigy, interview with Chris Salewicz, *Melody Maker*, June 6, 1981.

I remember I had this song called 'Machine' that was about this girl that reminded me of a machine. It was very explicit about her, er, parts. People seemed to find it very hard to take.

Prince, on "Machine", interview with Chris Salewicz, *Melody Maker*, June 6, 1981.

I only write from experience.
I don't plan to shock people.
I write about things I guess
people are afraid to talk
about.

Prince, on songwriting from experience, interview with
Tony Mitchell, *Sounds* magazine, June 6, 1981.

I think my father was kind
of lashing out at my mother
when he named me Prince.

Prince, on his regal name, interview with Dennis Hunt,
Los Angeles Times, December 21, 1980.

My dad left home for the first time and left his piano. He never let anyone play it before. So I taught myself songs from the television – *Batman*, *Man From UNCLE*. I learned to play them by ear.

Prince, on learning the piano, interview with Chris Salewicz, *Melody Maker*, June 6, 1981.

When the charts and awards are coming in your favour, they are the greatest thing in the world. When they are not working in your favour, they are absolutely meaningless.

Prince, on sales charts, interview with Chris Salewicz, *Melody Maker*, June 6, 1981.

My dad was in a jazz band, and I went to watch one of his gigs when I was about five. I was supposed to stay in the car, but I snuck out and went into the bar. He was up on stage and it was amazing. I remembered thinking, 'These people think my dad is great.' I wanted to be part of that.

Prince, on his father, interview with Robert Hillburn, *Los Angeles Times*, November 21, 1982.

I'm not saying I'm better than anybody else, but I don't feel like there are a lot of people out there telling the truth in their music.

Prince, on truth in music, interview with Robert Hillburn, *Los Angeles Times,* November 21, 1982.

"

I get $7 an album now.
If I sell 100,000 albums –
which they consider a failure
– I've got $700,000 in the
bank. That's cool. I've got
the money in the bank.
I'm holding the puppies,
you dig?

"

Prince, on money-making through album sales, interview
with Ben Edmonds, *Mojo* magazine, August 1998.

I want to make sure I'm dealing with the guy who hands you the money rather than the guy that hands you the bill, you know what I'm sayin'?

Prince, on controlling his finances, interview with Ben Edmonds, *Mojo* magazine, August 1998.

I always compare songwriting to a girl walking in the door. You don't know what she's going to look like, but all of a sudden she's there.

Prince, on songwriting, interview with Robert Hillburn, *Los Angeles Times*, November 21, 1982.

66

When I first got started in music,
I was attracted by the same things
that attract most people to this
business. I wanted to impress
my friends and I wanted to make
money. For a while, I just did it as
a hobby. Then it turned into a job
and a way to eat. Now I look on
it as art.

99

Prince, on his first attraction to music, interview with Robert
Hillburn, *Los Angeles Times,* November 21, 1982.

I realized after 'Dirty Mind' that I can get away with anything I want to get away with. All I have to do is be true to myself. I can make the records I want to make and still be OK. I feel free.

Prince, on being true to himself, interview with Robert Hillburn, *Los Angeles Times*, November 21, 1982.

You can say a bad word over and over again and sooner or later it won't be bad anymore if everybody starts doing it.

Prince, on a new type of revolution, interview with Barbara Graustark, *Musician*, September 1983.

Prince adored the colour purple as it reminded him of royalty and religion. It made him feel princely, he said. In the '90s, the Pantone Color Institute dedicated a unique shade of purple – called "Love Symbol #2" – to the Purple One, for his services to the colour.

However, his fascination with purple was also said to originate around his curiosity about the Judgement Day. "When there's blood in the sky – red and blue = purple… purple rain pertains to the end of the world and being with the one you love and letting your faith/god guide you through the purple rain," he told *NME*.

I think *Purple Rain* is the most avant-garde thing I've ever done. Just look at the singles 'When Doves Cry' and 'Let's Go Crazy'. Most artists won't try a groove like that.

Prince, on *Purple Rain*, interview with Lynn Normant, *Ebony* magazine, July 1986.

I'm not saying that I'm great or anything like that; I'm just saying that I'm an alternative. And I long to hear something else from everybody. There are a lot of talented people out there. I just don't think they go far enough.

Prince, on being alternative, interview with Lynn Normant, *Ebony* magazine, July 1986.

In the '60s, when everybody tried to be different, you had War and Santana, and Hendricks, and Sly, and James Brown, and they were all uniquely different. Now, everyone just jumps on what they think are the hottest sounds.

Prince, on musical recycling, interview with Lynn Normant, *Ebony* magazine, July 1986.

Money runs out, but music appreciates like real estate.

Prince, on money and music, interview with Steve Jones, *USA Today*, April 13, 1999.

It has been reported that Prince stayed awake for 154 hours – six days! – before his death.

If people think I'm insane, fine. I want people to think I'm insane. But I'm in control. I'm not playing anyone else's game. I don't care if people say I'm mad. It don't matter.

Prince, on his reputation versus control, interview with Andy Richardson, *NME*, March 11, 1995.

I have free will, and I'm ecstatic. There is no ceiling now – no limits. I can see the sky.

Prince, on being free, interview with Larry King, CNN, 1999.

66

You don't.

Prince, when asked, "So, how do you pronounce it?"
about his Love Symbol moniker, 1994.

A woman in climax.

Prince, when asked, "What is your idea of the ultimate guitar tone?", interview with *Guitar World* magazine, 1994.

"

Back when I was coming up, I didn't dress like anybody, I didn't look like anybody, I didn't sound like anybody. I still try to do that. Why do what everybody else is doing?

"

Prince, on being unique, interview with Anthony DeCurtis, *Rolling Stone* magazine, May 27, 2004.

I don't see myself as an icon. I don't see that. I didn't put myself on a pedestal. If I'm on a pedestal it's because other people have put me there.

99

Prince, on being put on a pedestal, interview with Andy Richardson, *NME*, March 11, 1995.

After I'm free from Warner Bros., it'll either be very quiet or very exciting. But it won't be in the middle. It'll be extreme. Life, I mean. It'll all be extreme.

Prince, on emancipation from Warner Bros., interview with Elysa Gardner, *Los Angeles Times*, July 14, 1996.

'Purple Rain' was the final song Prince ever performed live. It was the closing song at his final show in Atlanta, Georgia, on April 14, 2016 – a week before he died.

I really feel a need to school a new generation of musicians. Technology is cool, but you've got to use it as opposed to letting it use you.

Prince, on how to use technology, interview with Matt Lauer, MSNBC *The Today Show*, March 16, 2004.

Prince was renowned for not eating, often choosing to simply just smell his food, particularly when recording new material.

When he did eat though, his favourite meal was... spaghetti and orange juice (according to NME).

My name is the eye of me. It doesn't have a sound. It looks beautiful and makes me feel beautiful. Prince had too much baggage.

Prince, on his name change to Love Symbol, interview with Edna Gunderson, *USA Today*, November 12, 1996.

There's always been a dichotomy in my music: I'm searching for a higher plane, but I want the most out of being on earth.

"

Prince, on searching for more in music, interview with Edna Gunderson, *USA Today*, November 12, 1996.

Not to sound cosmic, but I've made plans for the next 3,000 years. Before, it was only three days at a time.

Prince, on looking to the future, interview with Edna Gunderson, *USA Today*, November 12, 1996.

I've gone several places in the world. And when I get back over that green and all those lakes, I feel peace. I think God puts you where you live for a reason, and I'll live in Minneapolis for the rest of my life.

Prince, on Minneapolis as his home, interview with Edna Gunderson, *USA Today*, November 12, 1996.

I never really needed approval for what it is that I do. I love that I'm appreciated and I love the respect that I get. But accolades and awards – you know it's all still big business.

Prince, on validation, interview with Matt Lauer, MSNBC *The Today Show*, March 16, 2004.

I'm a pretty open book.
People who know my music
I would say know me.

Prince, on being an open book, interview with Matt Lauer,
MSNBC *The Today Show*, March 16, 2004.

I make a lot of money on the road. I make $300,000 a night. You add that up and you can see why people want to put a rope around an artist. And sales of music is not as important as giving people a night they're going to remember. I'd just as well give the music away.

Prince, on music sales, interview with the *Irish Times*, September 19, 1998.

66

I do my music to excess.
Music, music, music – it's like
a curse that way. It can be
a curse. It's been like that
since I was seven years old
and my father left for the
last time. That's a lot to do
with it. My sister used food
and I used music.

99

Prince, on his obsession with music, interview with
Dan Glaister, *The Guardian*, July 3, 1998.

I had planned to do nothing in 1999 except reflect. I needed time off from the industry. Everyone said, 'But this is your year!' I stopped, I broke the pattern, I went away and didn't talk to anybody.

"

Prince, on his 1999 plans, interview with Edna Gunderson, *USA Today*, November 9, 1999.

Bowie and Madonna, even if it wasn't good, we still talk about them because it was something new. That's a beautiful word.

"

Prince, on his love of the new, interview with Anthony DeCurtis, *Rolling Stone*, May 27, 2004.

It has been revealed that the primary reason Prince contributed to the multi-million-selling soundtrack of Tim Burton's 1989 *Batman* film was because he fancied its star, Kim Basinger.

He hoped by writing the film's now-iconic songs he would get the chance to meet her. It worked… and the pair dated for a year.

Life is a symphony, and we
are all musicians. You are
either in harmony or not.

Prince, on life, interview with Barney Hoskyns, *Mojo*,
March 2000.

I won't speculate on where the music came from. I look back in awe and reverence. It's made me become courageous.

Prince, on the origins of his music, interview with Touré, *Icon* magazine, October 1998.

66

My goal is to excite and to provoke on every level.

99

Prince, on his ambitions, interview with Robert Hillburn, *Los Angeles Times*, November 21, 1982.